Indigenous Religions
(The Sun)

Hinduism
(Om/Aum)

Hinduism
(Swastika)

Zoroastrianism
(The Faravahar)

Judaism
(Menorah)

Judaism
(Star of David)

Jainism
(Ahimsa Hand)

Atheism/Agnostic/Humanism
(Encircled A)

Buddhism
(Wheel of Dharma)

Taoism
(Yin and Yang)

Atheism/Agnostic/Humanism
(An Atom)

Shinto
(Torii Gate)

Christianity
(Chi Rho)

Christianity
(Latin Cross)

Christianity
(Eastern Orthodox Cross)

Christianity
(Triquetra)

Christianity
(Celtic Cross)

Islam
(The Quran)

Islam
(Alhamdulillah)

Islam
(Star and Crescent)

Atheism/Agnosticism/Humanism
(The Happy Human)

Sikhism
(The Khanda)

Bahá'í Faith
(Nine-Pointed Star)

Wicca/Neopaganism
(Five-Pointed Star)

Advance Praise for
It's Considerate to Be Literate about Religion

"*It's Considerate to Be Literate about Religion* is a fun, compassionate, and lyrical journey into religious diversity. With whimsical prose and beautiful illustrations, Cunningham offers kindhearted depictions of religious differences alongside his invitation to appreciate their common moral commitments. **A must-have for childhood educators and families hoping to raise open-minded children!**"

—Matthew W. Hughey, PhD, Professor of Sociology,
University of Connecticut

"**Practical and intelligent**, this beautifully illustrated book offers many teachable moments. You are certain to broaden your religious literacy within its pages."

—Rosemary Klein, former president of The Baltimore Ethical
Society and founder of Three Conditions Press

"*It's Considerate to Be Literate about Religion* effectively addresses a most timely issue today. Its **thoughtful content, apt examples, and clear terminology** are complemented with excellent illustrations which further enliven the text and emphasize its message."

—Rev. John T. Grega, MA, STL, STM, ThM,
Director of Religious Studies, Character, and Service,
McDonogh School (retd.)

"A **learned, nuanced, and beautifully illustrated** introduction to key concepts in religious studies. Dr. Cunningham offers a potent remedy for our cultural disease of viewing the world's diverse religions in simplistic and reductive ways."

—J. F. Alexander, MA, JD, author of the spiritual adventure novel *I Am Sophia*

"In this important book by Dr. Steven Cunningham, the author builds on his previous works that explore the intersection of poetry and nomenclature to help us see a topic in a new and unique light. In his current work, Dr. Cunningham masterfully uses 'poemenclature' to make religious literacy an approachable topic for a wide population. This book provides a broad welcoming overview of different religious world perspectives. **It is a must-read for not only the young, but for people of all ages.**"

—Timothy M. Pawlik, MD, PhD, MPH, MTS, MBA, FACS, FSSO, FRACS (Hon.), Professor of Surgery, Ohio State University; scholar of religion

"Dr. Cunningham's contribution to the field of religious studies is **creative, accessible, and informative.** Most importantly, it addresses some of the most common misconceptions about religion and offers readers a more sophisticated and nuanced approach to understanding our diverse world."

—John Camardella, College World Religion, Prospect High School; Education Fellow, Religion in Public Life Program, Harvard Divinity School

"Cunningham's book is designed to promote religious literacy. Yet, its strength is in promoting curiosity, tolerance, dialogue, and understanding. He breaks down concepts in easy-to-understand language engaging the reader to want to learn more. He educates the reader through poetry, examples, and discussion. His ability to separate religion from the actions of persons who interpret their religion in violent ways is quite timely in promoting religious, cultural humility. **This is an essential reader for youth, parents, all adults** and particularly religious leaders who are uniquely positioned to promote healing and interfaith peace. The illustrations by Detwiler are excellent and add greatly to the book's content."

—Beth L. Muehlhausen, PhD, MDiv, BCC, LCSW; Sr. Researcher for Spiritual Care & Mission Integration, Ascension

"Dr. Cunningham's **wonderful book** does us a double service—it explains convincingly the necessity of religious literacy and it shows us how to be religiously literate. It is a hopeful and informative text, no matter the reader's religious point of view!"

—Rev. Christopher Dreisbach, PhD, Assisting Clergy, Old St. Paul's Episcopal Church, Baltimore, MD; Professor (part-time) of Moral and Systematic Theology, St. Mary's Ecumenical Institute of Theology

"As a high-school educator and mother of two, I cannot express how **deeply important** Cunningham's book is to our children and their future. Increasingly so, we live in an ever-changing world with complex issues that often revolve around religion because religion is embedded in our culture, politics, and society. Using wit and humor, Cunningham lays the foundation of religious literacy in a way that is easy enough for a middle schooler to understand, but entirely appropriate for high-school-aged readers and older. The carefully organized pauses and reminders throughout the book allow any parent an opportunity to further discuss concepts or for a child to ask their own questions. I cannot wait to read this with my own children!"

—Jeanne Shin-Cooper, MA, CRSE, National-Board-certified high-school educator, Buffalo Grove, IL

"Dr. Cunningham goes right to the questions to be asking to understand and nurture relationships of all kinds in our complex and challenging world. Yet, in pairing poetic whimsy with informative prose, he leads readers to and through these questions with imaginations opened and defenses lowered. From my perspective as a parent, a priest, and simply a person seeking to live thoughtfully and lovingly in diverse community, **this book is a gift**: offering a way into conversation and self-reflection."

—Rev. Jenni Ovenstone, MDiv, Sr. Associate Rector of St. Paul's Episcopal Church, Alexandria, VA

"This **beautiful and brief** educational book is as well written in prose as it is in poetry. Its clear and respectful message regarding religious diversity and inter-religious literacy weaves in social and political considerations without compromising religious nuance and personal integrity. I wholeheartedly recommend this book to every middle and high schooler—in short to all our youth in America who will be the inheritors of a beautiful land rich in heritage with growing diversity."

—Hasan Awan, MD, author of
Islam of the Heart: Living Religion with Presence

"A well-crafted and imaginative book assisting students to understand and address one of the critical issues facing our multireligious and multiethnic world—religious illiteracy. The eloquent poems and case studies, skillfully integrated into the text, are **brilliant**!"

—Ali S. Asani, PhD, Murray A. Albertson Professor of Middle Eastern Studies, Professor of Indo-Muslim and Islamic Religion and Cultures, Harvard University

"As Steven Clark Cunningham says, being religiously literate helps us understand one another, which helps us live together more harmoniously. The wonderful poems and thoughtful examples in his book make it **an excellent introduction to religious literacy**."

—George Fitchett, DMin, PhD, Professor, Department of Religion, Health & Human Values, Rush University

"This book provides indispensable nuance, compassion, and empathy to how diverse people grapple with humanity's enduring questions. It is **a beautiful introduction to how we should orient ourselves around religious literacy and difference**."

—Benjamin Sax, PhD, Jewish Scholar, Institute for Islamic, Christian, Jewish Studies, Baltimore, MD

"Steve Cunningham provides his young readers with a detailed and clearly written introduction to religious literacy. He manages to give serious depths to the topic while keeping each section manageably short and precise while continuously drawing his audience in. **Even a more experienced reader** will find his book a **well-balanced** combination of carefully chosen examples and important background facts that are well illustrated."

—Nina Redl, BCC, Chaplain, Lincoln, NE

"Now more than ever, religious literacy is needed in a world where 'othering' is far too common. Dr. Cunningham provides **useful insights and a sense of playfulness** to help readers gain insights that lead to understanding and move beyond mere tolerance: to curiosity, dialogue, and respect for religious difference. I highly recommend this book!"

—Rev. Ann Ritonia, MA, MDiv, Rector,
St. John's Episcopal Church, Ellicott City, MD

"*It's Considerate to Be Literate* is a wonderful example of what religious literacy is and how it can be fostered. The approach is thoughtful and educational and the illustrations beautiful. **Many will learn from it.**"

—Wendy A. Cadge, PhD, Barbara Mandel Professor of the Humanistic Social Sciences, Professor of Sociology, Dean of the Graduate School of Arts & Sciences, Brandeis University

"An engaging primer on the role of religion in social life. Dr. Cunningham's **clear prose and clever poems make challenging concepts accessible** to young readers—when's the last time you read YA poetry about Ludwig Wittgenstein and the definition of 'religion'?"

—Henry Goldschmidt, PhD, Interfaith Educator,
New York, New York

"Wherever we find ourselves—in a classroom, a workplace, a neighborhood—we encounter the presence of religious diversity. In his book, Dr. Steven Cunningham reveals a key way to avoid conflicts and tensions in our relationships: by becoming familiar with and learning about religion, especially religions that are not our own. The examples in the book clarify the various points he brings. Knowledge develops respect, tolerance, and acceptance of the 'other', exactly what our society needs now. Knowledge is power. I would **recommend this book to anyone, no matter what age**."

—Rabbi Ziona Zelazo, BsC; Assoc. Chaplain,
Valley Hospital, Ridgewood, NJ; Disaster Spiritual Care
Provider for the American Red Cross

"Dr Cunningham's book is **an absolute must-read for all clinicians and educators**. As we recognize the importance of providing care to all people with respect for diversity, equity, and inclusion, it is essential that respect for people's religious or spiritual beliefs and values be respected and honored in their care. This book is engaging, thoughtful, scholarly, and practical."

—Christina Puchalski, MD, OCDS, FACP, FAAHPM,
Professor of Medicine and Health Science; Executive Director,
The George Washington University's Institute for
Spirituality and Health (GWish)

"An **engagingly creative** approach that teaches the complexities of religion both in terms of appreciating its value and cautioning against its potential dark side."

—Peter Hill, PhD, Director, Office of Academic Research and
Grants; Professor, Psychology of Religion,
Biola University, La Mirada, CA

"Well-produced, accessibly written, and beautifully illustrated, **this book encourages the kind of well-informed engagement with religions that is all too rare, and yet increasingly a requirement of civilized encounter with others** in our time."

—Bruce D. Chilton, PhD, MDiv, Bernard Iddings Bell
Professor of Philosophy and Religion; Director,
Institute of Advanced Theology, Bard College

It's Considerate to Be Literate
about Religion

Poetry and Prose about Religion, Conflict,
and Peace in Our World

....

Book 3 in the Poemenclature Series

....

Dr. Steven Clark Cunningham
Illustrated by Susan Detwiler

Orange Hat Publishing
www.orangehatpublishing.com | Waukesha, WI

It's Considerate to Be Literate about Religion: Poetry and Prose about
Religion, Conflict, and Peace in Our World
Copyrighted © 2022 Dr. Steven Clark Cunningham
By Dr. Steven Clark Cunningham
Illustrated by Susan Detwiler
ISBN 9781645384366
LCN 2022905206

For information, please contact:

Orange Hat Publishing
www.orangehatpublishing.com
Waukesha, WI

To Dr. Diane Moore, one of the best educators I have ever met, who illuminated my path to religious literacy, and from whom I learned much of what is in this book.

Table of Contents

Poemenclature

Preface: Inventing a Word

This book is the third in the Poemenclature Series. As in my first two books (*Dinosaur Name Poems* and *Your Body Sick and Well: How Do You Know?*), in this book I continue the theme of combining poems and nomenclature.

Poems are collections of words that sometimes rhyme, often have rhythm, and always try to make you see things in a different way than you might otherwise.

Nomenclature is a word that refers to the act of naming things, especially in a particular discipline, such as the study of fossilized animals, called "paleontology" (like in *Dinosaur Name Poems*), or the study of the body, what goes wrong with it, and how we investigate the body and what goes wrong with it, called "medicine" (like in *Your Body Sick and Well: How Do You Know?*).

So, "poems" plus "nomenclature" gives us the **neologism**, "poemenclature"!

This Poemenclature book is structured much like my last two, starting with some nomenclature, but the topic is very different. Here, we are talking not about dinosaurs or the body, but instead about religion, and how we should best understand it; in other words, how to be *religiously literate*. Although this kind of nomenclature is different from naming dinosaurs or things in the study of medicine, the key principle is the same: if we don't clearly understand key terms, such as "religion" and "literacy," then it is hard to move forward to a better understanding of all the ways that religion shapes our world.

Each poem in this book is followed by a "Learn More" section with some words (like **neologism** above) boldfaced, indicating that they are defined in the Glossary.

A Note on Respect
for Religious Beliefs

I have striven throughout this book—in both tone and content, in both spirit and deed—to be respectful of religious beliefs. I have not, however, employed some practices often used in various religious traditions to express a specifically belief-based respect. This is partly because I am writing this book from a descriptive perspective, outside of any particular religious tradition, as opposed to writing from within a religion, in which case such practices would have a meaningful prescriptive sense (see, e.g., pages 6, 23, and 48 for more on this important distinction).

One practice I have not employed is that of avoiding use of the name of God. For example, many Jews and some Christians believe that "Yahweh" (a name for God) should not be written/pronounced, but instead believe it better to write/say "Adonai" (which means "Lord"). Another such practice is writing "G-d" instead of "God." Similarly, unlike many practicing Muslims, I have not used the common honorific "peace be upon him" following mention of the Prophet Muhammad. Many Muslims also believe that the words of the Quran, including the name of God (Allah), are so sacred and holy that one should be in a purified state to even touch the physical book, let alone use the book or its words disrespectfully. In a spirit of respect, I have chosen to use the calligram of the Arabic phase from the Quran and containing the name of God ("Alhamdulillah," meaning "Praise be to God") as a symbol of Islam, with the hope that my Muslim brothers and sisters will not find its use here inappropriate, offensive, or disrespectful.

Part I
Nomenclature

iteracy

Can you read?
Can you read books of poetry and prose?
How about religions? Can you "read" those?
Are you religiously literate?
That would be considerate!

Learn More about Literacy!

Everyone can read, right? Sadly, that is wrong: In the USA, 32 million adults (14% of the adult population) are illiterate. We do not know how many people, exactly, are *religiously* illiterate because it is harder to measure that, but we do see religious illiteracy all around us, as described below.

Just as a verbally illiterate person cannot very well understand words that are written on this page, and cannot *read* (in a literal sense) the language, so too a religiously illiterate person cannot *understand* religions that are all around them (cannot figuratively "read" the religions). So, religious illiteracy is, in a sense, *misunderstanding* religion. Indeed, the notion of literacy in this book is based on *understanding concepts* about religion, as opposed to merely *knowing facts* about various religions.[1] In fact, an understanding-based approach is recommended by the American Academy of Religion (see Reading Group Guide). Of course, it is important and useful to know facts about our world, including its religious aspects, but knowledge alone gets you only so far without *understanding* as well!

But what, exactly, you might be asking, do religious literacy and illiteracy actually look like? What are some examples of misunderstanding religion in our world? *Here are five aspects of religious literacy and some examples of how people can sometimes be religiously illiterate (often without even realizing it!):*

[1] For an example of a notion of religious literacy that stresses more knowing facts about religion than understanding the concepts, see Stephen Prothero's book *Religious Literacy: What Every American Needs to Know—and Doesn't* in the Suggested Further Reading section of the Reading Group Guide on p. 80.

Aspect #1: Distinguishing Inside vs. Outside

Practicing a religion "from the inside" is different from studying religion "from the outside"; in other words, a *devotional, spiritual, **theological*** approach to religion is different from a *religious-studies* approach; in still other words, a *prescriptive* approach (about how things should be, according to somebody) is different from an *analytical, descriptive* approach (about how things actually are for everybody).

Example: Sometimes, people may experience something and interpret it from within their own religious tradition without even realizing that they are doing so. They may even think that they are taking an objective, studious perspective from outside their religion. Some specific examples of this appear on page 44, where you'll encounter a Christian's view that the religion practiced in a particular Christian church that is classified as a hate group, the Westboro Baptist Church (WBC), is not "real" or "true" Christianity, and a Muslim's perspective that the Muslim terrorist organization **Al-Qaeda** is not practicing "real" or "true" Islam. While many Christians may reject WBC's interpretation of Christianity, and many Muslims reject **Al-Qaeda's** interpretation of Islam, that rejection is a prescriptive, **theological** stance taken *within* a religious tradition, not an objective description of the religion of WBC and **Al-Qaeda** from *outside* the religion. This does not mean that Christians and Muslims cannot reject terribly violent interpretations of their religions—they can and should—but the point I want to make here is that the rejection is a **theological**, devotional, prescriptive position that happens within the religion, not an objective description of the religion from outside the religion. To confuse these two stances is one manifestation of religious illiteracy (see the poem "*That*'s Not *My* Religion!" on page 44 and its "Learn More" section).

Aspect #2: Recognizing That Religions Are Internally Diverse and Dynamic

Religions are internally diverse, not uniform, and they change over time; not all Christians, Muslims, Hindus, **agnostics**, Buddhists, **atheists**, Sikhs, Jews, etc., believe and act like all the others in their same tradition.

Example: An example is the relatively common misunderstanding that religions are uniform and stable. Have you ever wondered what people of another religion believe? Maybe you are from a Christian family, and have wondered what Muslims believe? Or maybe you are from a family that leans agnostic, and have wondered what the different Christian **denominations** believe? It is easy to generalize that Christians all share the same "Christian" beliefs, that Muslims all share the same "Muslim" beliefs, and that all agnostics or athe-

ists share the same set of beliefs. However, this is untrue. Of course, there are some common themes and beliefs that people of a particular religious tradition or worldview share, but it would be a mistake, as the above example of WBC and **Al-Qaeda** illustrates, to think that there is no diversity within religions. There is much, indeed! As we will see on pages 26-27, religions are not **monolithic**; each religion has a lot of diversity of beliefs and practices.

And religions are not only internally diverse at a given moment, but they also change over time: they are different at different times in history. Christianity, for instance, demonstrates diversity among different **denominations** today, and most of the different varieties of Christianity today (all of which have different interpretations by different people) are also very different than those in the past, especially before the Reformation in the 16th century. Thinking that any religion is uniform or stable is a common way to be religiously illiterate. To say, for example, that "Christianity is a religion of peace" is to assume a homogeneity, or a uniform sameness, that does not really exist. To the contrary, much **violence** has happened in the past, and continues to happen, in the name of Christianity. We will see several examples of this in Part II.

Similarly, just as religions are complex in the sense that each one has many diverse interpretations, they are also complex in that they have both visible and invisible aspects. For example, even though each religion has certain concrete, visible **scriptures**, rites, rituals, and ceremonies, it would be religiously illiterate to miss the fact that religions are much more than just these visible, concrete manifestations.

Aspect #3: Understanding That, Unlike You, Religions Lack Agency

Religions are not **actors** with **agency**; in other words, they themselves do not *do* anything; instead, people do things. Although they do these things often in the context of one religious tradition or another, we must not forget that it is people, not religions, who *do* things.

> **<u>Example:</u>** Continuing with the **Al-Qaeda** example, this third kind of religious illiteracy was particularly common after the 9/11 terrorist attacks, and during the 2016 presidential election, when the religiously illiterate statement "Islam hates us" was often repeated. Islam, the religion, does not hate or love anyone; religions themselves do not *do* anything; rather, *people* do things. Some acts are peaceful, and some are violent. And importantly, *neither **peace** nor **violence** is inevitable*, but instead depends on our human **agency**, in other words, on what we humans *do*. Yes, violent things are often said and done in the setting of one religion or another, but this does not mean that *the religion* is doing the action, whether the actions are loving ones or hateful ones. In other words, unlike humans, religions are not **actors** with **agency**, as we will see in the poem "Actors with Agency?" and its "Learn More" section on pages 24-25.

Aspect #4: Appreciating Religious Influences

Religious influences exist in all parts of human public life and culture (sometimes obviously, sometimes not); religions are not merely private.

> **Example:** It is very common to think that religion is—or even can be—isolated to the private sphere. Thomas Jefferson, one of the greatest leaders of the USA, famously spoke of and advocated for a wall of separation between church and state, between the public and the private spheres. It is not always clear how people's private religious beliefs relate to public life, but it is increasingly clear to an increasing number of people—including many experts in the study of religion, society, and politics—that those beliefs do greatly impact public life, and that religious influences exist in all parts of human public life, even though the influences are not always obvious. As we will see in the poem "The Religious vs. the Secular" on page 16 and its "Learn More" section, religion is deeply embedded in human life: it is not just a place we sometimes go; it is the road we travel day to day.

Aspect #5: Recognizing Our Perspective, Our Situatedness

How we see or understand religions (and all things, really) depends a lot—more than we realize—on our unique, personal perspectives, which in turn depend on all the countless experiences that have shaped our perspectives, including our own personal histories and the histories of other individuals, and our communities, regions, and nations.

Example: It is very easy to forget that the only place from which we can see, experience, and understand the world and its religions is precisely where we happen to be! If you happen to be, for example, part of a persecuted Rohingya Muslim minority family in Myanmar (see pages 44-51), then what you "know" about the Buddhism of the majority may be very different from what you would "know" about Buddhism if you were part of a peaceful Buddhist family in Myanmar (see pages 44-51).

In other words, everything we "know" about the world we know from a particular perspective, or our particular situation, culture, family, religion, etc. We can think of this as our *situatedness*. It is easy to think that we can perform what historian of science Donna Haraway (see Reading Group Guide) has called the "god-trick," which is to be able to see everything from nowhere. But we cannot. On the contrary, all knowledge is situated. This does not, however, mean that anything can mean anything, as in extreme relativism. It does not mean that *all* interpretations are equally valid. Instead, it highlights the essential fact that everything we know and believe about our world depends on a particular social and historical context. It means that how we understand religion and religions depends greatly or entirely on our perspective, or our situatedness.

So, this book challenges you to ask yourself, "How religiously literate am I?" As we will see in Part III, there are many ways that a religiously literate person can avoid the mistakes in the above examples. But *what is religion*, anyway? Read on to find out!

hat is Religion?

Religion is hard to define—
Just ask Ludwig Wittgenstein.

He's a philosopher from Austria
Whose *brain* got nausea

Trying to define various things:
Not blocks, rocks, rings, and springs,

Words that name stuff you can touch,
but rather "truth," "soul," "mind," and such.

These things you can't see or weigh,
So, defining them, well, it's hard to say!

But then Ludwig saw (saving his sanity)
That some things are "defined" by resemblance in a family:

Like all games, religions are all in some way alike,
Having a *family resemblance*, if you like.

No single feature do they share,
Yet a certain similarity is there.

When Ludwig realized a word's meaning is its use,
From his nauseating confusion he finally got loose.

Religion is a word doing a job, like a tool.
Yes, it's about God, as a general rule,

But not always—it's even more, in this case:
It's a description of what in life actually takes place.

If you find a good priest, rabbi, imam, or brahmin,
They'll know it's also what separates sacred from common.

If we could ask Ludwig how he construes it,
He might say, "Well, it depends on how I use it!"

Learn More about Defining Religion

There are several ways to define things. For example, "triangular" is defined as "having three sides." All triangles have three sides, and all shapes with three sides are triangular. In other words, having three sides is both necessary and sufficient for being a triangle; it is *essential* to being a triangle. "Essentialist" definitions like this one are one type of definition, but they do not work well in all cases.

What about games, for example? That was the example that philosopher Ludwig Wittgenstein used to show his idea of "family resemblance." It is hard or impossible to come up with a list of what is both necessary and sufficient for being a game. Consider: What is needed to define a game? Having teams? But then solitaire would not be a game. Having a winner and a loser? But then catch would not be a game. There are board games, ball games, Olympic games, word games, puzzle games, video games, and many more. What they all have in common is hard to determine, so we cannot name all the *essential* conditions for games like we can for triangles.

However, we can define such things based on the ways that *they are similar to each other*. In other words, we can "define" things like games using a number of qualities that are typical of games (such as having teams, having a winner and loser, being enjoyable, and so on), even though not all games have every one of these qualities.

The fancy term for this kind of definition is **polythetic**. This is a really good way to define religions, too! Like games, religions do not have every single quality in common with each other, but they share many similarities.

For example, although the definitions for some common religions refer to God (like Christianity) or gods (like Hinduism), such **theist** concepts are rather foreign to other religions (like Buddhism) that do not really stress worship of God or gods. Despite this big difference, all three of these are still religions!

Therefore, we can "define" religion as follows: Religions are things that are made in response to the experienced world, by people who live within a culture and a society, and that are all similar to each other in a family-resemblance sort of way: nearly always involving shared experiences in a community and a shared set of beliefs about the **transcendent**, often including worship of God or gods, and typically stressing a separation between the **sacred** and the commonplace.

The Religious vs. the Secular

Some think that the secular
Is spectacular, molecular,

And to all things religious opposed,
Like a door against the cold is closed.

But not so if you zoom out openly;
There are things you miss when looking too closely.

Religion, it seems, is not discrete;
It's more like the street beneath your feet:

Wherever you go, to the pews or to skid row,
Religion paves the road; it surrounds us from head to toe.

Learn More about the Religious vs. the Secular

Religions are deeply involved in human life. They are part of human expressions and actions. They are embedded almost everywhere, interwoven with the fabric of our lives, even though it may not always be obvious. For some people, a world without religions is a goal, for others it is inconceivable, and for everyone it is a fact that religion is deeply embedded in public life. However, sometimes we want to talk about the absence of religion as an idea, and the word we use for this idea is "secular." But most places in the world are not truly secular, even when they describe themselves as such (see the poem "Syrian Civil War" and its "Learn More" section on pages 34-38). Rather, most places in the world are colored and shaped by religion, and the way they uniquely exist is in large part due to the religious history of the area.

Even people who are **agnostic** or **atheist** live in a world where religion is embedded in many, if not all, parts of society. This is why it is important for everyone to be religiously literate! The more we understand each other, the more harmonious we can live together, regardless of our differences.

cripture

Ancient words in black and white
Dance in shadows of candlelight,

From mouths of men in tribes
To the plumèd pens of scribes.

Before books, words on tongues survived,
Till finally on pages they arrived.

Though how, in the end, the stories got penned
Hides the ways they bend, first told aloud, friend to friend.

And even when first written down,
Words copied by hand changed from town to town.

A scribe, after all, is not a copy machine;
Scribes made changes, both seen and unseen,

Toiling beneath their candlelight,
Making gray seem black and white.

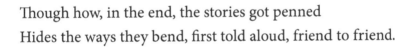

Learn More about Scripture

Scripture is the **sacred** (or holy) collection of writings of a religion. Although **scripture** is very important to many religions, religions are more than just these writings, or texts. One major reason for this is that the **sacred** texts require interpretation and are interpreted differently by different people. In fact, all texts—**scripture**, poetry, prose, nonfiction, news reports, comics, etc.—require interpretation (including, of course, the text you are reading right now!). You might even say that the *words do not speak for themselves.*

As odd as that may sound, it is true. For example, in the **Bible**, God parts the waters of the Red Sea, and Moses walks through the dry path between the parted walls of water. One way of interpreting that is literally: God actually caused the water to physically defy the laws of gravity. Another way to interpret this story is **metaphorically**, suggesting, for example, that God's help and guidance can be so powerful as to be like parting the sea.

However, do not think that this means that anything can mean anything! What it does mean is that when we read a text, we all bring to it our own unique set of experiences, feelings, expectations, hopes, fears, etc.: our situatedness. That is normal. This is true for both an individual student reading (interpreting) a textbook and for a religious community reading (interpreting) their **sacred** texts.

But where did **scripture** come from? Before books existed, people told their (hi)stories orally, passed on from person to person, from town to town, and from generation to generation. This is called the **oral tradition**. Back then, very few people could read or write, but much like today, religion was everywhere, in every part of society. This storytelling is how **scripture** was first communicated among people.

Some people nowadays assume that the people telling stories by **oral tradition** had such good memories that the stories were passed on unchanged, exactly as they were first told. We now know, however, that this is probably not true. Just think of the telephone game,

in which one person whispers something to the next person, and that person whispers what they heard to the next person, and so on. By the time the message has gone through several people over several minutes, the story changes a lot. If a story changes over just a few minutes among just a few people, think how likely it is that stories told orally year after year, decade after decade, likely changed a lot before they were written down (the earliest written versions of what Jesus did and said, for example, are manuscripts from several decades after his death). Likely or not, however, many people deeply believe that the words of the Christian **Bible** or the Muslim **Quran**, for example, have been passed from generation to generation perfectly, with no changes, from God to today's written **scripture**.

As more people learned to read and write, the first versions of **scripture**, such as the **Bible** and the **Quran**, were written down. However, they looked much different than they do now. For example, the words in the **Bible's New Testament** were written in all-capital Greek letters with no spaces between the words! Just imagine

how this sometimes caused confusion (an English example of this is "GODISNOWHERE," which could mean "God is now here" or "God is nowhere").[2] Similarly, the earliest versions of the Muslim **Quran** and the Jewish **Torah** were  also initially written mostly without modern punctuation marks, which today clarify meaning.

For many centuries prior to the invention of the printing press in the 15th century, copies of **scripture**—or any other text—had to be made by hand, one-by-one. People called scribes were in charge of making these copies, and it is well-known that, like all humans, they sometimes made errors. For example, we know that when copying the **New Testament** of the **Bible**, they made more changes to the text than there are words in the **New Testament** itself!

Many of these changes were unintentional and insignificant, like misspellings and confusions of look-alike words, but some scribes actually changed the meaning of the text. And some of those meaningful changes were done intentionally because the scribes wanted the stories to support one particular **theology**, or set of beliefs, over another one. Sometimes the politics of the time also affected how scribes changed the texts of **scripture**.

There are actually a lot of these intentional changes, which is not surprising when we consider that there were several different, competing versions of Christianity in the first centuries, and that each one had its supporters and opponents. Different people

---

[2] This example is borrowed from New Testament scholar Bruce Metzger, from his classic 1964 text *The text of the New Testament: Its Transmission, Corruption, and Restoration*. Full citation in the Suggested Further Reading section of the Reading Group Guide on p. 80.

in different Christianities each interpreted quite differently the meaning of Jesus's life and death.

As discussed in the introductory "Learn More" section following the poem "Literacy," there are two basic ways to look at this: 1) from the perspective of practicing a religion *within* that religion, and 2) from the perspective of studying religion from *outside* any particular religion. From the first perspective, one group may say that their way of understanding Jesus is **orthodox** while rejecting another group's way as **heretical**. The second perspective, however, accepts that both interpretations may be legitimate.

Eventually, one interpretation of Christianity emerged as the official, accepted understanding of Jesus, and everyone more or less agreed on an official collection of **scripture**, called the **canon**, to put in the **Bible**. Even today, there are slightly different versions of this one form of Christianity, and these slightly different forms are called **denominations** (such as the Catholics, and the Protestant denominations, such as the Episcopalians, the Lutherans, the Methodists, and many others).

See the poems "Literacy" and "*That*'s Not *My* Religion!" and their "Learn More" sections to learn more about this important distinction between seeing religions from these two perspectives, and see "The Holocaust" and its "Learn More" section for an actual example of how stories changed over time. Teachers, students, and parents may want to learn more about the changes made to the Bible in the book *Misquoting Jesus*, in the Suggested Further Reading section, and to consider some of the related Discussion Questions, both of which are found in the Reading Group Guide on page 80.

ctors
with Agency?

Agency? What is agency?
It could be a business
(like a travel agency)
Or part of the government
(like a consumer-protection agency),
But those are different from what I mean here.

Here, to have agency is to simply have the power
To *do* something, like plant a flower.

And what do you call people who have agency?
Actors, you do. And what do actors do?
They get on stage and perform on cue.
Ah, yes, but that's not what I mean.

Here, "actors who act," simply means people who *do*
(Like you!).
A person or a thing with the power to *do*
Is an actor, and actors have agency to act:
The power, quite simply, the ability, to *do!*

But do all persons and things have agency to act?
Well, most *people do* – that's a fact!
But *things*, not so much:
Don't expect agency from religions and such!

Learn More about Agency

Why all this talk about **actors** and **agency**? Because it is easy for people to make the mistake of thinking that religions themselves are actors with agency. For example, after the terrible 9/11 **terrorist** attacks, people said that "*Islam* hates us," or "*Islam* did this," instead of blaming the actual *group of people* (**al Qaeda**) who committed the attack. The mistake people made was saying that Islam, a religion, was an **actor** with **agency**. But religions are not **actors** with **agency**.

Religions (see the poem "What is Religion?" on page 12 and its "Learn More" section) are things made by people who live within a culture and a society, and most of these people do good things. Some do horrendous things, like hijack jet airplanes and fly them into skyscrapers, but it is important to recognize that people did this, not a religion. People who do such things may say that they do them for religious reasons (**ISIS** and other terrorist organizations do in fact say this), but that is simply because they have a particularly violent, aggressive, and unusual interpretation of their religion. Almost all other Muslims practicing Islam are **peace**-loving, ordinary people like you and me![3]

[3] Ali Asani's chapter in the Suggested Further Reading section of the Reading Group Guide on p. 80 has a good description of different Muslim understandings of Islam.

onolithic

What in the world is "monolithic"?

A one-brick Lego tower is: one you can't even start
(since it's all one piece) to build or take apart!

A smörgåsbord could be: one in which
Everything tastes the same, neither bland nor rich.

A film festival would be: one you could learn by heart,
Showing only *The Big Sleep* with Humphrey Bogart.

Being "monolithic" is soporific, dolorific, and nonspecific!
Does religion have much in common with it?

Learn More about the Diversity of Religions

Are religions **monolithic**? In other words, are they **homogeneous**, constant, and uniform? Or are they **heterogeneous**, changing, and diverse? What do you think?

Some people think, for example, that all Buddhists are **peaceful** because many Buddhist monks are, or that all Muslims are prone to **violence** because **Islamic** terrorists are. In reality, there are some very violent Buddhists and countless very peaceful Muslims (see the poem *"That's Not My Religion!"* on page 44 and its "Learn More" section). Religions are each internally diverse, not **monolithic**. They are interpreted differently by different people. Just a minute of reflection will convince us of this, since religions are made by groups of people, and all people, like all snowflakes, are different from each other.

Overreach
(Colonialism/Mission/Proselytizing)

Who, when they've found something cool, special, or rare,
Doesn't want everyone to share?

Who, when they see others in need,
Doesn't want to help them? Indeed!

We all do, of course, every man, woman, and child:
Share the gem, make the save, tame the wild.

The trick is to know which time is the charm,
And which time the good's outweighed by harm!

Learn More about Overreach

"Outreach" is a common term that refers to an organized attempt to provide services or education to some part of a community beyond the usual amount of attempting to engage with that community. The term has a generally positive sense today, like when a church reaches out to a homeless or poor part of their community to provide shelter, food, or supplies.

Colonialism, **missionary** work, and **proselytizing** are all types of outreach as well. As seen elsewhere in this book, **colonialism** generally has a negative sense because the harm caused by the colonizers (such as dividing communities, taking land or resources, etc.) can sometimes outweigh the good that they cause (such as providing education, health care, etc.). Unlike **colonialism**, which generally refers to a national endeavor, **missionary** work often refers to the work of smaller groups or individuals. Although both colonialism and missionary work imply going to a foreign place to cause a good change there, such endeavors are not always free of some self-interested motivation, and sometimes the overall effect for those in the foreign place is not good (for example, see "Nigeria: The Imam and the Pastor," "Syrian Civil War," "To Be in Myanmar," and "The Palestinian and the Israeli," and their "Learn More" sections).

Colonizers and **missionaries** often have explicitly religious goals also. For example, many Christian **missionaries** seek to **proselytize** (to convert) local people, who are sometimes seen as "wild" or "savage" by those **missionaries**, from their own native beliefs to the beliefs of Christianity. This is one way that colonization can divide communities: Converts to the new religion may oppose those who did not convert. This is the kind of outreach that has caused severe problems in places like Nigeria (see "Nigeria: The Imam and the Pastor" and its "Learn More" section on pages 40-43).

The desire to share with others what one thinks is wonderful can be so powerful that the sharing becomes an imposition, something that is forced upon others. The desire to impose Islam on others is sometimes referred to as **Islamism**, and people who do this are often called **Islamist**. The term **Islamist**, however, is also used by some people as simply synonymous with Islamic, which simply means having to do with Islam. The sense of "Islamist" referring to forcing Islam upon others applies to a very tiny minority of all Muslims. The overwhelming majority of Muslims do not want to impose their religion on non-Muslims.

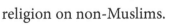

Part II
Examples of Conflicts

Syrian Civil War

Just a few years ago,
Syria was a wonderful place to go,

With as many people as New York or Taiwan.
(That's over a million times twenty-one!)

People like you and people like me,
People who notice a passing bumble bee,

Sauntered through millet meadow,
Inhaling sweet yellow avens of Aleppo.

Ten long years later,
    Where Syria was, now is a crater:

    A hollowed-out population,
        Half uprooted—
            Deracination.

        Humans like you, like me,
            But from firebombs, belief beatings,
                Crumbled kitchens having to flee,

    Dragging, trawling for pieces of their lives:
        Building dust, angry
            Gun-smoke hot
                In their lungs.

Learn More about Syria

According to Filippo Grandi in 2016, the United Nations High Commissioner for Refugees, the crisis in Syria was "the biggest humanitarian and **refugee** crisis of our time." Approximately 13 million people have been permanently pushed out of their homes and **deracinated** from their lives by the Syrian conflict. They now live in tents in Syria or in other countries, especially in nearby Turkey, Jordan, and Lebanon.

Aleppo is one of the oldest cities in Syria. Before the war, there were not only invaluable ancient ruins in the city, but there were also beautiful meadows on the outskirts, in which the yellow avens was a common wildflower (the scientific name of the yellow avens is *Geum aleppicum*, since "Geum" is an ancient Latin name for plants in the Avens group and "aleppicum" means "of Aleppo"). Now, sadly, this beautiful, ancient city and outskirts have largely been turned into modern ruins.

While the government in Syria considers itself **secular,** religion is very significant to the Syrian people and is embedded everywhere in Syrian life (see the poem "The Religious vs. the Secular" and its "Learn More" section on pages 16-17). In fact, despite being "**secular,**" the Syrian government is so infused with religion that the constitution requires that the president be a Muslim, and all

religious groups must register with the government. The control that the "**secular**" government tries to have on religion is so tight that it even bans Syrian Jews from communicating with Jews in Israel.

As with the conflicts in Nigeria, Myanmar, Israel-Palestine, and elsewhere, colonialism in Syria has created a situation that allowed conflict. In the case of Syria, whose borders were created by French colonialists after World War I, these borders created tension between different groups, and these tensions led to the civil war in Syria.

Syria has been ruled by the **authoritarian** and **militant** Ba'ath Party since 1971. From 1971 to 2000, Hafez al-Assad was the President of Syria, and his son Bashar al-Assad has been president from 2000 to the present. Both have been **authoritarian** leaders.

Some initial protests against this militant regime were led by Syrians who were inspired by the Arab Spring, which was a wave of demonstrations, protests, riots, and civil wars in North Africa and the Middle East that began in December of 2010 in Tunisia. In March 2011, prodemocracy protests in the southern Syrian city of Daraa were brutally crushed by the Syrian government, who used deadly force against the dissenters. This led to further protests nationwide, now demanding that the president resign. As the protests spread, the crackdown and violent suppression by al-Assad's government intensified. Opposition supporters therefore took up arms to defend themselves, and al-Assad labeled them "**terrorists**,"

vowing to crush them. The country then spiraled into civil war. Much **direct violence** rapidly escalated as hundreds of rebel groups sprang up in Syria, and various foreign powers took sides. The **violence** and chaos further increased with the rise of **terrorist** groups in Syria, such as **ISIS** and **Al-Qaeda**.

The book you are reading is written for youth (and adults), and this poem was inspired by Syrian **refugee** youth. (In fact, it was the protest graffiti of youth in Daraa, Syria that helped start the civil war.) Unfortunately, in the past several years of civil war, many of those young people have lost not only their books but also their homes, their families, and for many, their own lives.

igeria: The Imam and the Pastor

Nigeria is east of Benin and west of Cameroon,
In the tropics, so warm most any afternoon.
It's south of Niger and north of the Atlantic,
Where the mouth of the river splays out gigantic,
And huge nets gather flocks of wild tuna
To be converted to food and sold in Kaduna.

The tuna in Kaduna know no God,
But the humans there do believe in God.
In which God they believe, however, depends,
And sadly, they often can't make amends.
While the Christians praise Yahweh and Muslims praise Allah,
The animals don't care, whether tuna, chimp, or impala.

But the humans care so much they'll kill each other,
Sometimes even fathers, mothers, sisters, and brothers,
Nigerian versus Nigerian. The worst is Boko Haram,
Terrorists who enforce their beliefs with a bomb.
What can stop the cycle of violence,
Fear, hatred, and religious intolerance?

Look at the example of Imam Ashafa and Pastor James,
Religious leaders fighting each other amid the flames
That ravaged Kaduna. But one day, Ashafa had a change of heart;
He heard anew words of old, and his angry shell fell apart.
He asked forgiveness…Pastor James was suspicious at first,
Since by now he had come to expect the worst,

Seeing only what he expected to see.
Yet Ashafa persisted and Pastor agreed:
His book also taught to love and forgive,
To hold onto hatred like water in a sieve.
Now together they lead, their differences a wraith,
Showing their followers the best way is interfaith.

Learn More about Nigeria

Located on the west coast, Nigeria is the most populated country in Africa. Almost everybody is religious, about half Christian and half Muslim. A small percentage practice **indigenous** religious traditions, also known as African traditional religions, of which there are countless different kinds. Although the **indigenous** traditions were the only religions in Nigeria originally, the nation is now largely divided by religion due to British **colonialism**, with Muslims mostly in the north and Christians mostly in the south.

Kaduna is a state in the middle of Nigeria just north of the above-mentioned divide, and it has suffered many deep-seated conflicts. These conflicts generally involve religious groups, especially the notorious terrorist group **Boko Haram**, which was

founded in 2002 as an offshoot from a particularly extreme and violent interpretation of Islam.

In many of these conflicts, religious leaders such as Imam Ashafa and Pastor James have participated in an **interfaith** approach, which has helped to ease tension. They have been models of success by striving not just to *tolerate* each other as persons of differing faith but to *embrace* each other's personhood and faith, thereby increasing **cultural peace** (the opposite of **cultural violence**). You can learn even more about the Imam and the Pastor by watching their documentary (shorturl.at/cquOZ) and about yourself by considering the Discussion Questions in the Reading Group Guide (page 80).

hat's *Not* *My* Religion!

At Westboro Baptist Church,
On the corner under a birch,

Christians hold signs high,
Yelling at passersby:

"God hates the USA
And hates all who disobey!"

That's *not* my *religion, says the Christian pigeon!*

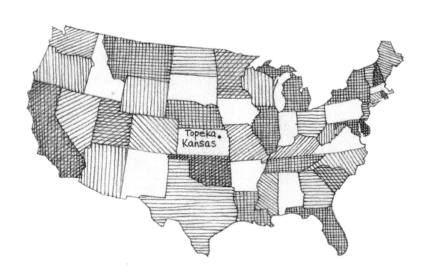

Burma, now known as Myanmar,
Is where red-robed Buddhist monks are.

At ninety percent, a huge majority,
for most Buddhists, peace is a priority.

But some don't follow peaceful rules,
Like in 2013, when they burned Muslim homes, mosques, and schools.

That's *not* my *religion, says the Buddhist pigeon!*

On 9/11, in New York, New York,
Half a million Muslims abstained from pork,

Said their prayers, helped their neighbors,
Went peacefully about their labors.

But nineteen hijacked four airplanes,
Killing 3,000, sent pain running through our veins.

That's *not* my *religion, says the Muslim pigeon!*

Learn More about *My Religion*

Westboro Baptist Church (WBC) is a Christian hate group in To-
peka, Kansas that is known for hate speech against homosexuals,
Catholics, Muslims, Jews, and others.

Myanmar (pronounced MEE-an-mar) is a country in Asia. Formerly called Burma, it is bordered by India, China, Thailand, and the
Bay of Bengal. Almost everyone (nearly 90%) in Myanmar is Buddhist. One minority is a group of Muslims called the Rohingya (pronounced ro-HINGE-ya) in western Myanmar, and **violence** against
the Rohingya has led many people to call them the most persecuted
minority in the world. **Violence** against the Rohingya is generally

seen as a religious conflict between Buddhists and Muslims, but many other factors are also at work, as explained on page 51 in the "Learn More" section of "To Be in Myanmar."

The 9/11 (2001) attack was the worst terrorist attack in world history. Muslim terrorists killed about 3,000 people in the USA by hijacking jet planes and crashing them into the Twin Towers in Manhattan. Following 9/11, there was an increase in **cultural**, **structural**, and **direct violence** against Muslims, including prejudice, discrimination, and physical attacks, respectively, especially in the USA. Some people vented their anger on innocent people who happened to share the "same" religion with the terrorists (Islam), albeit generally with drastically different interpretations. Even some innocent non-Muslims whom attackers thought looked like Muslims were assaulted.

In all three cases from this poem, a few people interpreted their religion in violent ways that led to conflict, but those interpretations would be rejected by the vast majority of people who share in those religious traditions. Sometimes it is tempting to say, for example, that the Christians in WBC are not "true" Christians or are practicing a "misinterpretation" of Christianity; that the violent Buddhists are not "true" Buddhists; and that **Al-Qaeda** (the Muslim **terrorist** organization that committed the 9/11 attacks) is practicing a "misrepresentation" of Islam or is not practicing "true" Islam. Does this temptation lead us in the right direction?

The answer to that question is complicated and has a lot to do with the first aspect of religious literacy mentioned in the "Learn More" section of the introductory poem, "Literacy" (page 4). From *within* a particular religion (for the people who practice and interpret the religion), it is entirely appropriate to reject, for example, WBC as not "true" Christianity, or the anti-Rohingya

people as not "true" Buddhists, or **Al-Qaeda** as not "true" Muslims. A great many people certainly do reject these interpretations. However, from *outside* of any of these religions (for people who study religion and different religions without necessarily taking part in them, like you are right now), it is important to recognize that there is no such thing as the one, single, correct, "true" interpretation of a religion. Rather, all religions are internally diverse and interpreted very differently by different people, often peacefully, but sometimes very violently.

So, while it is appropriate to draw critical attention to these violent religious groups—and indeed, one would be right to do so—it is important to remember that sometimes, writing off such extremist groups, discounting them, "**othering**" them, simply saying "*that's* not *my* religion," can prevent us from asking important questions. For example, what is it about the social, economic, and political context that brings people to WBC? What allows Buddhists to act violently? What attracts recruits to **Al-Qaeda**?

When we **other** these groups, we might fail to ask those key questions and so fail to understand the complexity of their religious interpretations and the complexity of the protean ways that each interpretation interacts with different communities. Such failures to understand make it more difficult to prevent unnecessary **violence** in the world. Reducing any individual or group to an "**other**"—an incomprehensible other, an intolerable other, an alienated other—artificially simplifies their multiple, complex stories to a **single story**. The danger of what Chimamanda Ngozi Adichie has called the "**single story**" (see Reading Group Guide) is that it is incomplete, it emphasizes how we are different rather than how we are similar, and it makes it easy for **cultural violence**

to occur. Part of becoming **religiously literate** is being aware of the many stories that each person and group has.

We saw an example of a **single story** above, in the "Learn More" sections for "Literacy" and "Actors with Agency?" in the statement *"Islam hates us."* This statement, in addition to the problematic ascription of agency to Islam, is problematic because it reduces the many complex stories of each Muslim to this **single story**, which produces **cultural violence**. Single stories about groups—including WBC, the Rohingya and Buddhists who persecute them, and **Al-Qaeda** and young men who are recruited to them—tend to ignore all the complex social, cultural, political, and economic factors that are at work in these groups.

To Be in Myanmar

How would it feel to be blessed among the Burmese?
Thanakha drying cool on your face in the breeze.

How would if feel to be Muslim in Myanmar?
Village on fire, beating your body, must run away far.

Learn More about Myanmar

Myanmar, formerly called Burma, is a Buddhist-majority nation in Southeast Asia. Although it was the richest country in Asia when it attained independence in 1948, it has now become one of the poorest in the region after decades of military rule. Only about a third of people have electricity, and malnutrition and disease are very common.

Thanakha is a paste made from the root of trees that grow abundantly in Myanmar. It has been used on the skin for thousands of years, not only for cosmetic reasons but also because it gives a cooling sensation and offers some protection from the sun.

A small percentage of Myanmar's population is Muslim (probably less than 5%, but accurate census numbers do not exist). Most of these

Muslims are Rohingya Muslims. Over one million Rohingya live in Rakhine, an area in Myanmar along the coast of the Bay of Bengal and the Bangladesh border. Despite living here for many generations, they have not been granted citizenship by either Myanmar or Bangladesh. **Violence** against the Rohingya Muslims has been long-standing.

If that were not bad enough, it has escalated in recent years, spreading even to other Muslim minorities. Even the main hospital has refused to treat these Muslims. The perpetrators of this **violence** against the Rohingya Muslims are almost uniformly Buddhist **nationalists** who are afraid that the Rohingya Muslims will take over their country. This conflict is generally seen as a religious one, but, as with all conflicts, there are several different factors at work.

Many experts think that the hostility between Burmese Buddhists and the Rohingya Muslims and other minorities is partly caused by British **colonialism**. One strategy of British **colonialism** was to give power to the minorities in order to diffuse control. This led to a collapse of the traditional organization of power and authority. Because religion is so deeply embedded in the lives of both the Burmese and the Rohingya, Burmese Buddhist **nationalism** arose from a fear that the Buddhist identity was threatened by the Rohingya Muslims.

The Holocaust

When did the Holocaust start?
When did everything fall apart?

When six million people were killed,
How and by whom and when was that willed?

Was it when the first of those six million died?
Was it when something broke in Hitler, deep inside?

Was it January 30th, 1933,
When Germany gave him the key?

Was it because Adolf's art career didn't flower?
Was it that World War I left Germans sour?

Was it the assassination of Archduke Franz Ferdinand,
Which led Austria-Hungary to declare war on Serbia's land?

Was it when Edgardo Mortara was baptized?
(To save his soul, his Jewishness was exorcised.)

Was it in 325, at the First Council of Nicaea,
When Christians arrived and liked the idea

Of not using the Jewish calendar for Easter
Since Jews, they thought, deserved a kick in the keister

For being Jesus-Christ-smiters,
According to the Gospel writers?

When, oh, when did the Holocaust start?
When, oh, when did everything fall apart?

Learn More about the Holocaust

The term "**holocaust**" literally means "sacrifice by fire" and generally refers to a huge destruction or slaughter. When capitalized, it refers to the Jewish **Holocaust**, the persecution and murder of six million Jews in Nazi Germany (**direct violence**), which was systematic and sponsored by the Nazi government (**structural violence**), due in large part to anti-Jewish sentiment fomented by Hitler (**cultural violence**).

The Nazi party came to power in Germany in January, 1933, when Adolf Hitler was appointed Chancellor of Germany by President Paul von Hindenburg. When von Hindenburg died, Hitler declared himself to be the Führer (German for "leader" or "guide," essentially now used to refer to a tyrant or dictator).

Hitler believed that Germans were racially superior and that the Jews, by virtue of being Jews, were "inferior." He felt that they were an alien threat to the German community, even though Jews were a minority with German citizenship who had been living there for centuries.

Where does something like the **Holocaust** begin? Although it is a difficult question to answer—indeed, many scholars have spent their careers trying to answer it—it is an important question to ask.

Many people think that World War I, which is thought to have been triggered by a flammable combination of **nationalism, imperialism**, and **militarism** ignited by the assassination of Archduke Franz Ferdinand, left Germany in a vulnerable state in which Nazism could arise.

But would the **Holocaust** have happened if there was not anti-Jewish sentiment already? Where did that come from? That is another question that is difficult to answer but important to ask. Certainly, there have long been conflicts between Jews and other groups (just as there have been conflicts that occurred among non-Jewish groups).

One example is that of Edgardo Mortara, a sick Jewish boy who was violently taken from his weeping mother and father by Roman officials on June 23, 1858, because it was discovered that 4 years earlier, when he was very sick, his 14-year-old Catholic nursemaid (the equivalent of a babysitter or nanny) panicked and baptized him, motivated by the Christian religious **doctrine** of Original Sin (which says, in part, that if you are not baptized before you die then you cannot go to heaven). The rationale for taking the child from his parents was based on two religious beliefs: 1) that the baptism made the child permanently Christian, and 2) Christian children were forbidden from being raised by Jews.

Over 1,500 years earlier, in the year 325, the First Council of Nicaea met in Nicaea (which today is called Iznik, located in Turkey). One of the items on the agenda was to separate the calculation of the date of Easter from the Jewish calendar, which had been used for this purpose until then. According to The **Epistle** of the Emperor Constantine (recorded by the theologian Theodoret), it was wrong to follow the calendar of the Jews because they were the "murderers of our Lord," "our adversaries," "out of their minds," and "utterly depraved" (see Reading Group Guide).

Indeed, even the Christian **New Testament** places an increasing amount of blame for the death of Jesus on the Jews (and a decreasing amount of blame

on the Romans) as the decades passed following his crucifixion, which most scholars date at Passover time around the year 30. This trend is seen in both the **canonical** and **noncanonical** Gospels, as described below.[4]

Even though historically, Jesus's execution was almost certainly the decision of the Roman governor Pontius Pilate, in the earliest Christian **Gospel**, Mark, written about year 70 CE (40 years after the crucifixion), Pilate and the Jewish Temple leaders are shown to decide *together* that Jesus should be crucified.

Later, sometime in the 80s and 90s CE, the Gospels Luke and Matthew were written. In Luke, the blame shifts further toward the Jews, as Pilate is portrayed as not wanting to execute Jesus, declaring him innocent. In the end, his hand is forced by the Jewish leaders, so he orders Jesus to be crucified. Matthew's **Gospel** goes even further and actually has Pilate not only declare Jesus innocent but also symbolically wash his hands of the death, declaring that he is innocent, and has the Jews say "His blood be upon us and our children." The author of Matthew apparently wanted to show that the Jewish people accepted the responsibility for Jesus's death. In the

last of the **canonical Gospels** (John), written about 15 years later, or about the year 100 CE, Pilate actually hands Jesus over to the Temple leaders to be crucified, and *they* are the ones then who crucify him.

In later, **noncanonical Gospels**, such as the **Gospel** of Peter and the Pilate **Gospels**, the blame is shifted

[4] See also Ehrman (2005) and Aslan (2013) in the Suggested Further Reading section of the Reading Group Guide on p. 80.

even more from Pilate to the Jews. In some later traditions, Pilate even converts to Christianity and becomes a Christian saint.

The audience for whom the **Gospels** (in particular, Luke) were written was largely Romans living throughout the empire. The authors, of course, wanted to appeal to their audiences, and they effectively showed that the Roman state was increasingly innocent of Jesus's death. Therefore, it is not surprising that the stories of the crucifixion increasingly emphasize a Jewish role, and deemphasize a Roman role, in Jesus's death.

(In addition to being an important part of understanding anti-Semitism, this review of the changing **Gospel** narrative shows how **scripture**, like religions themselves, changes over time. See also the "Learn More" section for "Scripture" on pages 20-23).

Some people think that this resulted in the anti-Jewish sentiment in early Christianity, later called anti-Semitism, which grew stronger as Christianity spread across the world. Whatever the cause, anti-Semitism reached its terrible peak in Nazi Germany with the Jewish **Holocaust**.

The Palestinian and the Israeli

The Palestinian and the Israeli
Are at each other's throat daily.

Fighting forever is not what they planned
When coming with claims to that land.

Both descendants of the storied Abraham,
Yet each hearing from the other just flimflam.

So, there they are, stuck in the fight,
No durable end in sight.

Learn More about Israel-Palestine

Israel-Palestine is a narrow strip of land west of Jordan, east of the Mediterranean Sea, north of Egypt, and south of Lebanon and Syria. At various times through history, it has been called Israel, Palestine, Canaan, The Holy Land, and The Promised Land. There has been conflict there between the Israeli Jews and the Palestinian Arabs for nearly 100 years, or since the end of the Ottoman Empire. Prior to this, as occurred in medieval Spain (see "Al-Andalus" and its "Learn More" section on pages 63-64), Christians, Jews, and Muslims lived in comparative **peace** together in Israel-Palestine.

Prior to World War I, Israel-Palestine was part of the Ottoman Empire. Following World War I, after the collapse of the Ottoman Empire in 1923, this area became controlled by Britain. People there began to develop a strong sense of **nationalism**: many Arab Muslims had a Palestine **nationalism**, and many Jews had a Jewish **nationalism**, called **Zionism**. As more Jews arrived, some fleeing persecution in Russia and elsewhere, some for religious reasons, and some for economic or other reasons, tensions with the Arab Palestinians increased. Those Palestinians had already lived there for several centuries and so thought of the land as their home. Then, in the 1930s, Britain began to limit immigration, which led to Jewish militias forming to oppose both the local Palestinian Arabs and the British rule.

Because of the **Holocaust** (See "The Holocaust" and its "Learn More" section), even more Jews fled to Israel-Palestine, and much of the international community supported this since Jews needed a safe place to go. The British asked the United Nations, which had just formed in 1945, to help make a solution. Israel-Palestine was divided into two separate, oddly shaped, roughly equal states in 1947: a Jewish state (Israel) and an Arab state (Palestine).

The Jewish Israelis agreed, but the Palestinian Arabs did not, unsurprisingly, since to them it seemed like more **colonization**, with Western powers trying to take their land. In 1948, the Arab-Israeli war broke out. In 1949, the Jewish Israelis won this war, claiming even more land than the UN gave them. This created a huge **refugee** crisis, with hundreds of thousands of Palestinians being forced to flee their homes.

In 1967, the Six-Days War broke out between Israel and neighboring Arab states. Israel won this war also and gathered even more territory. In 1978, USA President Jimmy Carter hosted the Camp David Accord, after which Israel gave some of the land back to the Palestinians but continued to occupy certain parts of Israel-Palestine, such as the West Bank (named as such because it is west of the Jordan river). More and more Jews moved in, and they even settled in the West Bank, despite this being considered illegal by the international community.

There are several reasons why Jewish Israelis feel that this is their rightful land even though someone else is living there. Some of those reasons are based in their **scripture**, such as chapter 13 of the book of Genesis, in which God says to Abraham that he is giving the land to Abraham. However, there are additional reasons: historical reasons (they believe that they were there first to settle there and never fully left), humanitarian reasons (they needed a place to live safely since they were persecuted elsewhere), and political reasons (the United Nations partition resolution of 1947, etc.).

The Palestinians started an uprising in 1987, which began with boycotts of Jewish products but eventually became violent. It was called The Intifada. More **militant** groups began to form, such as Hamas, which thought that other Palestinians were too soft and too **secular**. A second Intifada started in 2000 and was even more violent than the first one, lasting until 2005. Since then, there has been little to no sign of **peace** in the area.

Throughout the conflict, each side claims to be merely defending itself against the aggression of the other, but in reality, both sides have continually failed to understand the other's perspective as legitimate.

It is important to note that not all Israelis are Jews (e.g., there are Muslim Israelis), and not all Palestinians are Muslim (e.g., there are Christian Palestinians). Similarly, not all Muslims are Arabs, and not all Arabs are Palestinians. Currently, Israel-Palestine is divided into two main areas that correspond with the 1947 lines described above.

This dispute is complex and is partly about land, but it is also about politics, economics, and **theology**.

l-Andalus

From 711 to 1492,
Before you-know-who sailed the ocean blue,

Most Christians, Muslims, and Jews
Didn't have to choose

Between fleeing with their true faith
And staying with false-religious wraith.

In Arabized Spain, all were free to pray,
To stay, or to go as they liked, any day!

Learn More about Al-Andalus

The medieval period in Spain (then called al-Andalus) was known for being a time of not only particularly good religious **tolerance** but also great advancements in science and technology (what we would today refer to as STEM [science, technology, engineering, and mathematics]).

There is good evidence that the three main **monotheisms** (Christianity, Islam, and Judaism) in al-Andalus not only tolerated each other but also embraced aspects of each other's culture. These three religions are also called the Abrahamic religions because they all embrace **scripture** going back to the prophet Abraham in the **Old Testament** (Christianity), the **Quran** (Islam), and the **Torah** (Judaism). Even in al-Andalus, however, life was not all rosy and fair; there was still some religious discrimination, as in most human societies, including our society today, and it's essential to remember that this form of violence, like all violence and all peace, is not inevitable, but rather depends on our human agency, including mine and yours!

Part III
Appendix:
Putting It All
Together

Ways to Be Religiously Illiterate

1   Confuse **Inside vs. Outside**

DON'T think that particular Christians (or Muslims, Jews, etc.) are not practicing the one, true Christianity (or Islam, or Judaism, etc.)...

...**because** they may interpret it differently than others do, and you may prescriptively reject that interpretation, but that rejection happens inside the religion; from a descriptive, outside approach, there are multiple legitimate perspectives.

2   Think That Religions Are **Uniform and Stable**

DON'T think that religions are simply the rites, rituals, and ceremonies that are commonly performed; or that they are defined by their scriptures; or that they are monolithic and unchanging...

...**because** religion is much more complex than this; scripture is important to many religions, but religions are more than scripture; religions are very dynamic, changing over time, from place to place, and from person to person.

3   Think That Religions Have **Agency**

DON'T think of religions as things that can do something, or in other words, as actors with agency; do not see the actions of individuals or communities through the lens of their religion alone...

...**because** religions do not *do* anything; rather, people who interpret religions different ways do different things; people are more than their religions, and the reasons people do things are rarely just religious alone, but instead should be seen through the multiple lenses of their social, political, and cultural life.

4   Fail to Appreciate **Religious Influences**

DON'T think that religion is merely a private issue and otherwise separate from public life...

...**because** appreciating religious influences is a critical part of understanding modern human affairs locally, nationally, and globally.

5   Fail to Recognize Your Perspective, Your **Situatedness**

DON'T think that any of us is able to perform the "god-trick," i.e., see everything from nowhere...

...**because** all beliefs and knowledge about our world, including what we believe and know about and within religions, depend on our particular social, historical, and political context.

How to Be Religiously Literate

1 Distinguish **Inside vs. Outside**

DO learn to tell the difference between devotional, prescriptive, theological expression of religion, which occurs within a religion, versus the analytical, descriptive study of religion from outside the religion.

(See pages 6, 19, and 44.)

2 Recognize That Religions Are Internally **Diverse and Dynamic**

DO recognize that religions are internally diverse, not uniform or monolithic, and there are many interpretations of each religion. Understand that religions and their narratives evolve and change with the times.

(See pages 7, 12, 19, 24, 26, 29, 40, 44, and 63.)

3 Understand That Religions Lack **Agency**

DO remember that, unlike you, religions are not actors with agency; they do not *do* anything; instead, *people* do things. There are many examples of peace and violence in the world, but neither is inevitable; instead it depends on human agency, on your agency, and mine.

(See pages 9, 19, 26, 52, and 58.)

4 Appreciate **Religious Influences**

DO see and appreciate that religion is embedded in and influences all dimensions of culture, as opposed to being purely private and separate.

(See pages 10, 16, 19, 34, and 50.)

5 Recognize Your Perspective, Your **Situatedness**

DO recognize that all our knowledge and beliefs about the natural world and the **supernatural** are *situated*; recognize that religion too is situated and interpreted in a particular way, depending on one's context.

(See pages 10-11, 12, 19, and 40.)

Glossary

Actor: someone who acts, or does, something.

Agency: 1) the capacity, condition, or state of acting or of exerting power; 2) a person or thing through which power is exerted or an end is achieved. <u>Etymology</u>: *agens,* past participle of *agere* to do, act.

Agnostic: 1) a person who does not have a definite belief about whether God exists or not; 2) a person who does not believe in or is unsure of something. <u>Etymology</u>: *a-* without + *-gnōstós* known.

Allah: "God" in Arabic (the language) and in Islam (the religion).

Al-Qaeda: the **militant, fundamentalist,** extremist, faith-based **terrorist** organization that committed the 9/11 terrorist attacks.

Atheist: a person who believes that God does not exist. <u>Etymology</u>: *a-* without + *-theos* god.

Authoritarian: a leadership style based on the principle of strict obedience of people to the leader at the expense of the people's freedom. <u>Etymology</u>: *auctoritas* opinion, decision, power.

Bible: the book of **sacred** writings (**scripture**) of Christians, which includes the **Old Testament** and the **New Testament.**

Boko Haram: a **militant, Islamist** organization, considered by many to be **terrorists,** whose main target is the **secular** Nigerian government. "Boko Haram" means "Western education is forbidden" in the Hausa language.

Canon: 1) an authoritative list of books accepted as holy **scripture** (e.g., the **Bible**); 2) the authentic works of a particular writer; 3) an officially approved or accepted group or body of related works.

Canonical: having to do with a **canon.**

Colonialism: control by one nation (like the British empire) over an area or people (like Nigeria) who depend on the colonizers.

Cultural violence/peace: see "**violence.**"

Daesh (or Da'ish): another term for **ISIS**; an Arabic acronym formed from the initial letters of one of the group's names in Arabic.[5]

Deracination: the state of being removed or separated from a native environment or culture; literally "uprootedness." Etymology: *de-* remove + *-racine* root.

Denomination: a religious body made up of a number of people with similar beliefs. For example, Methodists and Baptists are different Protestant denominations of Western Christianity. Etymology: *de-* something derived from + *-nominare* to name.

Direct violence: see "**violence.**"

Doctrine: a set of ideas or beliefs that are taught or believed to be true; **dogma.**

Dogma: a belief or set of beliefs that are accepted by the members of a group without being questioned or doubted.

Epistle: a letter adopted as a book of the **New Testament.** More generally, any formal or elegant letter. Etymology: *epi-* on + *-stellein* to send.

Fundamentalism: a movement or attitude stressing (often excessively) strict and literal adherence to a set of basic principles.

---

[5] "**Daesh**" is the term for "**ISIS**" preferred by some people because "**ISIS**" implies they are a legal state, which they are not. "**Daesh,**" by contrast, challenges the legitimacy of the group due to the negative connotations of the word. Additionally, "**Daesh**" also sounds similar to an Arabic verb that means to tread underfoot, trample down, or crush something, which they do. The words we use matter!

Gospel: a book or message telling of the life, death, and resurrection of Jesus Christ. The four **canonical** Gospels in the **New Testament** are named Matthew, Mark, Luke, and John, but there are a number of **noncanonical** Gospels that were not chosen to be included in the biblical **canon.** More generally, also refers to the message of Jesus Christ, the kingdom of God, and salvation. <u>Etymology:</u> *gōd-* good + *spell* tale (often translated "good news").

Heretical: 1) adhering to a religious opinion that is contrary to church **dogma**; 2) having to do with a departure from accepted beliefs or standards.

Heterogeneous: made up of parts that are different from each other. <u>Etymology:</u> *heter-* other, different + *-genos* kind.

Holocaust: 1) a sacrifice consumed by fire; 2) a complete destruction involving extensive loss of life, especially by fire; 3) often capitalized: the mass slaughter of European civilians, especially Jews, by the Nazis during World War II; 4) a mass slaughter of people. <u>Etymology:</u> *hol-* complete, total + *-kaustos* burnt.

Homogeneous: made up of parts that are all the same or similar to each other. <u>Etymology:</u> *hom-* same, similar, alike + *-genos* kind.

Illiterate: 1) being unable to read or write; 2) Being unfamiliar with the fundamentals of a particular field of knowledge, like music (musically illiterate) or religion (religiously illiterate). <u>Etymology:</u> *il-* not + *-litteratus* learned, educated.

Imperialism: the actions by which one nation is able to be more powerful than others by controlling other nations, usually smaller or weaker nations.

Indigenous: produced, growing, or living naturally in a particular place. <u>Etymology:</u> *indu-* in, within + *-gignere* to beget, produce, procreate.

Interfaith: involving persons of different religious faiths, often with the purpose of working together in a respectful, collaborative manner. Ideally, this is not simply **tolerance** of those of differing faiths but an embracing of them as fellow humans.

ISIS: an acronym standing for "Islamic State of Iraq and Syria," also known as Islamic State of Iraq and the Levant (ISIL) or simply Islamic State (IS). ISIS is a **militant, fundamentalist**, extremist, faith-based, **terrorist** organization that violently attacks others for what they claim to be explicitly religious reasons (namely, their perception that others fail to embrace their Islam and the oneness of God as they interpret it). See also **Daesh**.

Islamic: having to do with Islam.

Islamist: 1) having to do with the faith, **doctrine**, or cause of Islam; 2) a reform movement advocating the reordering of government and society in accordance with laws prescribed by Islam.

Metaphor: a figure of speech in which words that usually mean one thing are used to describe another thing, thus suggesting a similarity between the two things (as in "you are my sunshine" or "the ship plows the sea").

Militant: 1) being at war; 2) aggressively active, especially in a cause.

Militarism: the opinions or actions of people who believe that a country should use military methods, such as aggressive force, to gain power and to achieve its goals.

Mission: 1) a group sent to a foreign country to have discussions or to provide training or help; 2) a group, a place, or a work of **missionaries**.

Missionary: someone sent on a mission, often to spread a religious faith among unbelievers or to engage in charitable work with religious support.

Monolithic: 1) formed or made up of a single piece of material without joints, consisting of a single unit; 2) constituting a massive and often rigid whole; 3) exhibiting or characterized by often rigid and unchanging uniformity. <u>Etymology</u>: *mon-* one + *-lithos* stone.

Monotheism: the belief that there is only one God. <u>Etymology</u>: *mon-* one + *-theos* god.

Nationalism: loyalty and devotion to one's country, often including the belief that it is better and more important than other countries.

Neologism: a new word or expression. <u>Etymology</u>: *neo-* new + *-logos* word.

New Testament: the second part of the Christian **Bible**, which contains the **canonical Gospels** and **Epistles** in addition to the book of Acts of the Apostles and the book of Revelation.

Noncanonical: see "**canonical**."

Old Testament: the first part of the Christian **Bible**, which contains the books of the Jewish **canon** of **Scripture**.

Oral tradition: the stories, beliefs, etc. that a group of people share and pass on by word of mouth.

Orthodox: conforming to established **doctrine**, especially in religion. <u>Etymology</u>: ortho- right, correct + -doxa opinion.

Other [verb]: to view (a people or a group, etc.) as excluded, intrinsically different from, and alien to oneself.

Peace: see "**violence**."

Pentateuch: the first five books of Jewish and Christian **scriptures**. <u>Etymology</u>: *penta-* five + *-teuchos* tool, vessel, book.

Polythetic: sharing a number of characteristics of a group or class, none of them essential for membership in the group or class in question. Etymology: *poly-* many + *-theticos* placed.

Proselytize: 1) to convince someone to change religious faith; 2) to try to get new people to join one's cause or group. Etymology: *pros-* near + *-ēlytos* went.

Quran: the book (also written "Qur' an" and "Koran") composed of **sacred** writings (**scripture**) accepted by Muslims as revelations made to Muhammad by **Allah** through the angel Gabriel.

Refugee: a person who has been forced to leave their country in order to escape war, persecution, or violence. Etymology: *re-* + *-fugere* to flee.

Sacred: 1) worthy of religious worship; 2) very holy; 3) relating to religion; 4) highly valued and important.

Scripture: a body of writings considered **sacred** or authoritative.

Secular: 1) not spiritual or not religious; 2) of or relating to the state rather than the church.[6]

"Single story": an overly narrow, focused narrative, as of a person or group of people, that is **stereotypical** and therefore incomplete.

Stereotype: a mental picture that is held in common by members of a group and that represents an oversimplified opinion, prejudiced attitude, or uncritical judgment of a person, group, place, etc.

Structural violence/peace: see "**violence.**"

---

[6] Although this is a correct *dictionary* definition of "secular," in practice, religions are often deeply implicated in human expressions and actions, even when we may not notice. See the poem "The Religious vs. the Secular" and its "Learn More" section on pp. 16-17.

Supernatural: having to do with existence beyond the visible, observable universe, especially having to do with God, gods, demigods, spirits, or devils.

Torah: 1) the teachings and law contained in Jewish **scripture** and other **sacred literature** and **oral tradition**; 2) the **Pentateuch**.

Terrorism: the use of terror, generally very violent and destructive acts, as a means of achieving a goal.

Theist: a person who believes that God exists or that many gods exist. Etymology: *theos* god.

Theology: 1) the study of religious faith, practice, and experience, especially the study of God and of God's relation to the world; 2) a distinctive body of theological thought, opinion, or belief. Etymology: *theos-* god + *-logos* word, study.

Tolerance: 1) ability to put up with something harmful or unpleasant; 2) sympathy for or acceptance of feelings, habits, or beliefs that are different from one's own.

Transcendent: beyond the limits of ordinary experience; beyond comprehension. Etymology: *trans-* across, through, over, beyond + *-scendre* to climb.

Violence, types of (direct, structural, and cultural): a way of thinking about violence described by Johan Galtung, widely considered to be the "Father of Peace Studies."[7] He developed a three-pronged typology of violence that shows how different factors can combine in cultures to allow for violence (or peace) to be accepted as normal. The three types are direct, structural, and cultural violence, and they are layered one on top of the other:

---

[7] See Johan Galtung's classic 1990 article in the Suggested Further Reading section of the Reading Group Guide on p. 81.

Direct violence. This is violence you can easily see—natural violence like earthquakes, personal physical violence like stonings, and deprivational violence like enslaving are some examples. Other examples are punching, pushing, killing, maiming, bullying, sexual assault, and emotional manipulation.

Structural violence. This is the less obvious violence underlying direct violence. It is the social institutions and systems—the social structures—that can give rise to direct violence. This is sometimes called systemic violence, and it prevents some groups from having equal access to opportunities, goods, and services needed for basic human needs. Such structures can be formal, as in laws that enforce marginalization (such as slavery in the US and elsewhere, or Nazi rules against Jews in Germany). But structures can also be active culturally, even without actual laws formally supporting them (such as limited access to health care for the Rohingya Muslims in Myanmar).

Cultural violence. Most important but most subtle, this is the violence that underlies direct and structural violence. Cultural violence is any aspect of a culture that can be used to make direct and structural violence look or feel right, or at least not wrong. In other words, it legitimizes the other types. Examples include the belief that Africans and Jews were inferior (which made slavery and Nazism seem okay to many people).

Galtung used the metaphor of earthquakes to illustrate these three types of violence. As you may know, earthquakes occur along fault lines, which are cracks in Earth's crust where tectonic plates meet. In this metaphor, the fault line is the prominent condition (like the social norms of cultural violence) which allows for the movement of tectonic plates in relation to one another (structural violence), which gives rise to earthquakes (direct violence).

Zionism: an international effort working at first for a Jewish homeland in Palestine and then later for the support of Israel.

Reading Group Guide

Discussion Questions

Questions and topics for discussion are available at
https://stevenclarkcunningham.net/poetry.

Suggested Further Reading for Parents/Guardians, Teachers, and Students[8]

Adichie, Chimamanda Ngozi. (2009, July). *The danger of
a single story* [Video]. TEDGlobal. https://www.ted.com/
talks/chimamanda_ngozi_adichie_the_danger_of_a_
single_story?language=en.

American Academy of Religion. (2021). *AAR religious literacy
guidelines*. American Academy of Religion. Retrieved June
11, 2021 from https://www.aarweb.org/AARMBR/
Publications-and-News-/Guides-and-Best-Practices-/
Teaching-and-Learning-/AAR-Religious-Literacy-
Guidelines.aspx?WebsiteKey=61d76dfc-e7fe-4820-a0ca-
1f792d24c06e.

Asani, A. S. (2011). Enhancing religious literacy in a liberal arts education
through the study of Islam and Muslim societies. In J. Shephard, S.
Kosslyn, & E. Hammonds (Eds.), *The Harvard Sampler* (pp. 1-31).
Harvard University Press.

Aslan, R. (2013). *Zealot: The life and times of Jesus of Nazareth*. Random House.

Ehrman, B. D. (2005). *Misquoting Jesus: The story behind who
changed The Bible and why*. HarperCollins.

---

[8] Some of these sources are created for the general public. Others are more academic and
written by scholars for other scholars, such as those published by university presses or in
academic journals, but all are worth a look for those interested in learning more!

Galtung, J. (1990). Cultural violence, *Journal of peace research 27(3)*, 291-305. https://www.galtung-institut.de/wp-content/uploads/2015/12/Cultural-Violence-Galtung.pdf.

Harvard Divinity School (2021). Harvard's *Religious literacy project*, now joined with the Religion in Public Life program at Harvard Divinity School. https://rpl.hds.harvard.edu/what-we-do/our-approach.

Haraway, D. (1991). "Situated knowledges: The science question in feminism and the privilege of partial perspective" in *Simians, Cyborgs, and Women: The reinvention of nature* (p. 191). Routledge.

Menocal, M. R. (2003). *The ornament of the world: How Muslims, Jews, and Christians created a culture of tolerance in medieval Spain.* Back Bay Books.

Metzger, B. M. and Ehrman B. D. (2005). *The text of the New Testament: Its transmission, corruption, and restoration* (4th edition). Oxford University Press.

Moore, D. L. (2007). *Overcoming religious illiteracy: A cultural studies approach to the study of religion in secondary education.* Palgrave.

Moore, D. L. (2008). *Overcoming religious illiteracy: A cultural studies approach.* University of Illinois. Retrieved April 29, 2021 from http://worldhistoryconnected.press.illinois.edu/4.1/moore.html.

Omer, A., Appleby, R. S., and Little, D. (2015). *The Oxford handbook of religion, conflict, and peacebuilding.* Oxford University Press.

Theodoret of Cyrus. (c. 325 C.E.). The epistle of the emperor Constantine, concerning the matters transacted at the council, addressed to those bishops who were not present (recorded by the theologian Theodoret). https://biblehub.com/library/theodoret/the_ecclesiastical_history_of_theodoret/chapter_ix_the_epistle_of_the.html.

Acknowledgements

No good book is written in a vacuum by a single, truly independent author. Rather we are all situated in protean relationships that shape who we are, what we think, and what we write. Accordingly, there are countless people I should thank for their invaluable contributions to this book, but given the impossibility of thanking everyone, I would like, first and foremost, to thank my best friend and wife, Myriam, not only for her unfailing support and astonishing strength through the rigors of my surgical training—which is already a lot to ask, not to mention especially while she also worked full time and we had four young children at home—but also now for her accepting support of my decision to go back to school to pursue a master's degree in religion at this relatively late stage in my surgical career. This book would not be possible without her support allowing me to follow my passion. As a poet, I would like to thank my community of fellow poets, including friends, and poetry mentors and role models, especially Rosemary Klein and Michael Salcman, from whom I have learned much, although I know that I still have much to learn; I hope that any failure to meet their high standards has not been so egregious as to embarrass by naming them. Of course, I owe a great debt to all of my professors, TAs, and mentors at Harvard, especially Diane Moore, from whom I have learned so much of what is in this book. To all those who so generously gave their time and energy to read earlier drafts of the manuscript, I am extremely grateful, especially to Jim Alexander, Ana Cunningham, John Grega, Suleiman Hani, Matthew Hughey, Shannon Mullen, Jeanne Shin-Cooper, and Pepper Smith. About the editorial team at Orange Hat Publishing, I cannot say enough! Shannon Ishizaki, Lauren Blue, Hanna Cook, Pam Parker, and the indefatigable Kaeley Dunteman have been simply awesome. And, although her talent is obvious from her illustrations, what is not as obvious is the remarkable kindness, collegiality, and generosity of spirit that Susan Detwiler brought to this project, much like she did with our last book, *Your Body Sick and Well*. Thank you all!

About the Author

Dr. Steven Clark Cunningham was born in Denver, Colorado. After graduating from Creighton University with majors in chemistry and Spanish, he attended medical school at George Washington University in Washington, DC. Having completed his residency in general surgery at the University of Maryland and a fellowship in surgery of the liver and pancreas at Johns Hopkins University, he now serves as Director of Pancreatic and Hepatobiliary Surgery as well as Director of Research at Ascension Saint Agnes Hospital in Baltimore, MD. He is currently completing his master's degree in religion at Harvard University.

He has served as a contributing editor of *Maryland Poetry Review*, and his poems have appeared in that journal. In addition, his work won the literary arts contest sponsored by the magazine *The New Physician*. His poems have also appeared in *Chimeras*, *Word-House Baltimore's Literary Calendar*, and in the anthologies *Function at the Junction #2*, *Pasta Poetics*, and *Poems for Chromosomes*.

It's Considerate to Be Literate about Religion is this third book of poetry. His first full-length book of children's poetry, bilingual in English and Spanish, was *Dinosaur Name Poems / Poemas de Nombres de Dinosaurios* (Three Conditions Press, 2009), which won the 2009 Moonbeam Award in both the Children's Poetry and the Spanish Language categories. His second book, *Your Body Sick and Well: How Do You Know?* (Three Conditions Press, 2020), was awarded 1st Place in Children's Nonfiction at the 26th Annual CIPA EVVY Awards Contest, sponsored by the Colorado Independent Publishers Association, and a Gold Medal in the 14th Annual Moonbeam Awards. It was also a Finalist in the 14th Annual National Indie Excellence Awards.

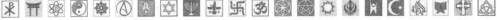

About the Illustrator

Susan Detwiler has illustrated several award-winning books for children, including *Your Body, Sick and Well: How Do You Know?* and her seventh title for Arbordale publishing, *Bat Count: A Citizen Science Story.* She is the author/illustrator of *Fine Life for a Country Mouse*, a picture book published by Penguin Random House in 2014. Her illustrations have appeared in children's magazines, and have been used for puzzles, games, and greeting cards. Susan and her artist husband live in Baltimore. She is a member of the MD/DE/WV chapter of the Society of Children's Book Writers & Illustrators.

Indigenous Religions
(The Sun)

Hinduism
(Om/Aum)

Hinduism
(Swastika)

Zoroastrianism
(The Faravahar)

Judaism
(Menorah)

Judaism
(Star of David)

Jainism
(Ahimsa Hand)

Atheism/Agnostic/Humanism
(Encircled A)

Buddhism
(Wheel of Dharma)

Taoism
(Yin and Yang)

Atheism/Agnostic/Humanism
(An Atom)

Shinto
(Torii Gate)

Christianity
(Chi Rho)

Christianity
(Latin Cross)

Christianity
(Eastern Orthodox Cross)

Christianity
(Triquetra)

Christianity
(Celtic Cross)

Islam
(The Quran)

Islam
(Alhamdulillah)

Islam
(Star and Crescent)

Atheism/Agnosticism/Humanism
(The Happy Human)

Sikhism
(The Khanda)

Bahá'í Faith
(Nine-Pointed Star)

Wicca/Neopaganism
(Five-Pointed Star)